P9-CRF-695

SHARK ZONE

TIGER SHARK

by Deborah Nuzzolo

Reading Consultant:
Barbara J. Fox
Reading Specialist
North Carolina State University

Content Consultant:
Jody Rake, member
Southwest Marine/Aquatic Educators' Association

CAPSTONE PRESS
a capstone imprint

Blazers is published by Capstone Press,
151 Good Counsel Drive, P.O. Box 669, Mankato, Minnesota 56002.
www.capstonepub.com

Copyright © 2011 by Capstone Press, a Capstone imprint.
All rights reserved.
No part of this publication may be reproduced in whole or in part, or stored in a retrieval system,
or transmitted in any form or by any means, electronic, mechanical, photocopying, recording,
or otherwise, without written permission of the publisher.
For information regarding permission, write to Capstone Press,
151 Good Counsel Drive, P.O. Box 669, Dept. R, Mankato, Minnesota 56002.

 Books published by Capstone Press are manufactured with paper
containing at least 10 percent post-consumer waste.

Library of Congress Cataloging-in-Publication Data
Nuzzolo, Deborah.
  Tiger shark / by Deborah Nuzzolo.
      p. cm.—(Blazers shark zone)
  Summary: "Describes tiger sharks, their physical features, and their role in the ecosystem"—
Provided by publisher.
  Includes bibliographical references and index.
  ISBN 978-1-4296-5415-9 (library binding)
  1. Tiger shark—Juvenile literature. I. Title. II. Series.

QL638.95.C3N896 2011
597.3'4—dc22   2010024839

Editorial Credits

Christopher L. Harbo, editor; Juliette Peters, designer; Eric Mankse, production specialist

Photo Credits

Alamy/Stephen Frink Collection, 5, 6–7, 9; Visuals&Written SL/Mark Conlin, 20–21;
    WaterFrame, 16
Peter Arnold/Biosphoto/Rotman Jeffrey, 26–27; Doug Perrine, 12; Stephen WONG, 25; .
    WILDLIFE, 22
© SeaPics.com/James D. Watt, cover, Doug Perrine, 10–11
Shutterstock/A Cotton Photo, 28–29; Undersea Discoveries, 15, 19

Artistic Effects

Shutterstock/artida; Eky Studio; Giuseppe_R

Printed in the United States of America in Stevens Point, Wisconsin.
092010   005934WZS11

TABLE OF CONTENTS

CHAPTER 1

TIGER OF THE SEA

A shark with faint stripes and spots swims silently through the sea. Its triangle-shaped fins cut through the water. Its powerful tail pushes it toward a shallow reef.

reef—a strip of rock, coral, or sand near the surface of the ocean

The shark circles the reef. Suddenly, it smells its **prey**. With a sweep of its tail, it darts in the direction of its prey. The tiger shark is on the hunt.

prey—an animal hunted by another animal for food

CHAPTER 2

DANGEROUS HUNTER

Tiger sharks are large, powerful hunters. They can grow 14 feet (4.3 meters) long. They weigh up to 1,400 pounds (635 kilograms).

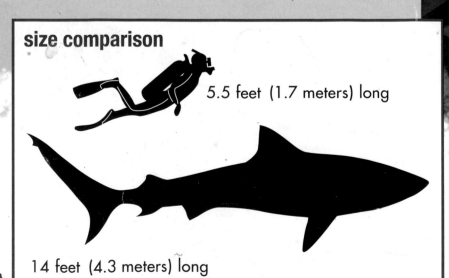

size comparison

5.5 feet (1.7 meters) long

14 feet (4.3 meters) long

SHARK FACT

The largest tiger shark ever caught was more than 24 feet (7 m) long. It weighed 6,856 pounds (3,110 kg).

Young tiger sharks have bold, black spots and **vertical** stripes. These markings fade as the shark grows. The spots and stripes almost disappear on adults.

vertical—straight up and down

A tiger shark's wide mouth holds many rows of jagged teeth. The shark shakes its head back and forth to slice through large prey. Its teeth are strong enough to crack a sea turtle's shell.

SHARK FACT

Tiger sharks often lose front teeth when they eat. New teeth in the back of the jaw move up to replace them.

Tiger sharks are excellent nighttime hunters. Their large, black eyes have special **reflective** plates. These plates help tiger sharks see in dark or cloudy water.

SHARK FACT

A shark's eyes are on the sides of its head. This position allows sharks to see in nearly all directions.

reflective—acting like a mirror

Tiger sharks hunt seals, dolphins, sea turtles, fish, and squid. But they are not picky eaters. They will also eat birds, other sharks, and even garbage.

SHARK FACT

License plates and old tires have been found in tiger shark bellies.

CHAPTER 3

WARM WATER WANDERER

Tiger sharks swim in all of the world's oceans. They usually hunt in warm, shallow water. At night they hunt near reefs and lagoons. During the day, tiger sharks move to deeper water.

Tiger Shark Range

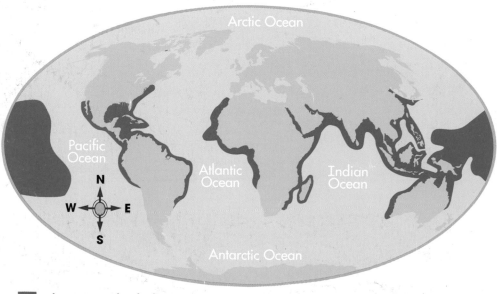

where tiger sharks live

lagoon—a shallow pool of seawater separated from the sea by a narrow strip of land

Tiger sharks live where they can find food and the right water temperatures. Some tiger sharks stay in one place all year. Others travel from island to island across the sea.

SHARK FACT

Tiger sharks swim up to 20 miles
(32 kilometers) per hour.

Tiger sharks help keep oceans healthy. As **predators**, they keep animal populations from growing too large. They also help keep the ocean clean by eating litter.

predator—an animal that hunts other animals for food

CHAPTER 4

RESPECTED PREDATOR

Tiger sharks are curious creatures. They sometimes approach swimmers in shallow water. Attacks are rare. But people must be careful swimming in places tiger sharks have been spotted.

SHARK FACT

Although attacks are rare, tiger sharks are the second most dangerous shark to people. Only the great white shark attacks people more often.

People harm tiger sharks more often than tiger sharks harm people. Some people catch tiger sharks for sport. People also catch tiger sharks for their meat, skin, fins, and liver.

A tiger shark's liver is rich in vitamin A.
People use it to make vitamin oil.

Tiger sharks are also caught by accident. People who fish for tuna or swordfish sometimes hook a tiger shark instead. Although tiger sharks are not **endangered**, heavy fishing has hurt their numbers.

endangered—at risk of dying out

Glossary

endangered (in-DAYN-juhrd)—at risk of dying out

lagoon (luh-GOON)—a shallow pool of seawater separated from the sea by a narrow strip of land

litter (LIT-ur)—garbage scattered around carelessly

predator (PRED-uh-tur)—an animal that hunts other animals for food

prey (PRAY)—an animal hunted by another animal for food

reef (REEF)—a strip of rock, coral, or sand near the surface of the ocean

reflective (ri-FLEK-tiv)—acting like a mirror

vertical (VUR-tuh-kuhl)—straight up and down

Read More

Doubilet, David, and Jennifer Hayes. *Face to Face with Sharks.* Washington, D.C.: National Geographic, 2009.

Goldish, Meish. *Tiger Sharks: Blue Blenders.* Disappearing Acts. New York: Bearport Pub., 2010.

MacQuitty, Miranda. *Shark.* DK Eyewitness Books. New York: DK Pub., 2008.

Internet Sites

FactHound offers a safe, fun way to find Internet sites related to this book. All of the sites on FactHound have been researched by our staff.

Here's all you do:

Visit *www.facthound.com*

Type in this code: 9781429654159

Check out projects, games and lots more at
www.capstonekids.com

Index